Congressional Research Service

Understanding China's Political System

Susan V. Lawrence
Specialist in Asian Affairs

Michael F. Martin
Specialist in Asian Affairs

May 10, 2012

Congressional Research Service

7-5700

www.crs.gov

R41007

CRS Report for Congress ─────────────
Prepared for Members and Committees of Congress

Summary

This report is designed to provide Congress with a perspective on the contemporary political system of China, the only Communist Party-led authoritarian state in the G-20 grouping of major economies. China's Communist Party dominates state and society in China, is committed to maintaining a permanent monopoly on power, and is intolerant of those who question its right to rule. Nonetheless, analysts consider China's political system to be neither monolithic nor rigidly hierarchical. Jockeying among leaders and institutions representing different sets of interests is common at every level of the system. A test of the political system will come later this year, when the Communist Party plans to usher in a new set of top leaders at its 18th Congress. China's last two major political transitions, in 1997 and 2002, unfolded relatively smoothly. This year, the political system has been shaken by the recent ouster of a senior Party leader, Bo Xilai. The unity of the remaining leadership remains unclear.

The report opens with a brief overview of China's leading political institutions. They include the Communist Party and its military, the People's Liberation Army; the State, led by the State Council, to which the Party delegates day-to-day administration of the country; and the National People's Congress (NPC), China's unicameral legislature. The NPC is meant to oversee the State Presidency, the State Council, the Supreme People's Court, the Supreme People's Procuratorate (China's public prosecutor's office), and the military. In practice, the legislature is controlled by the Communist Party and is able to exercise little oversight over any of those institutions.

Following the overview, the report introduces a number of distinct features of China's formal political culture and discusses some of their implications for U.S.-China relations. Those features include the fact that China is led not by one leader, but by a committee of nine; that provincial leaders are powerful players in the system; that the system treats statements by individual leaders as less authoritative than documents approved by committee; and that ideology continues to matter in China, with the Communist Party facing vocal criticism from its left flank each time it moves further away from its Marxist roots. Other themes include the importance of meritocracy as a form of legitimization for one-party rule, and ways in which meritocracy is being undermined; the introduction of an element of predictability into elite Chinese politics through the enforcement of term and age limits for holders of public office; the Chinese system's penchant for long-term planning; and the system's heavy emphasis on maintaining political stability. The next section of the report discusses governance challenges in the Chinese political system, from "stove-piping" and bureaucratic competition, to the distorting influence of bureaucratic rank, to factionalism, corruption, and weak rule of law, as highlighted by the case of the blind legal advocate Chen Guangcheng. A text box discusses the case of the disgraced senior leader Bo Xilai.

The second half of the report is devoted to detailed discussion of China's formal political structures—the Party, the military, the State, the National People's Congress, a consultative body known as the China People's Political Consultative Conference, and China's eight minor political parties, all of which are loyal to the Communist Party. Also discussed are other political actors who are playing a role in influencing policy debates, including the media, big business, research institutes, university academics, associations, societies, and grassroots non-governmental organizations. The report concludes with a discussion of prospects for political reform, noting that while China's Premier Wen Jiabao has called for undefined political reform, Party policy is to reject vigorously the notion of a multi-party system, separation of powers, a bicameral legislature, or a federal system, on the grounds that all are unsuited to China's conditions.

Contents

Figures

Tables

Contacts

Introduction

This report is designed to provide Congress with a perspective on the contemporary political system of China, the world's second largest economic power, one of five permanent members of the United Nations Security Council, and the only Communist Party-led authoritarian state in the G-20 grouping of major economies.[1] By introducing some of the distinct features and governance challenges of China's political culture, the report aims to help Congress understand the ways in which political actors in China interact, or in some cases, fail to interact, with implications for China's relationship with its neighbors and the world. By introducing some of the leading political institutions and political actors in China, the report aims to help Congress understand where Chinese interlocutors sit within the Chinese political system, gauge their relative influence, and judge the authoritativeness of their statements with respect to official policy. Where appropriate, the report also seeks to highlight ways in which China's political culture affects official Chinese interactions with the U.S. government.

The **Chinese Communist Party (CCP or Party)** has been in power in China for more than six decades, a record of longevity that rivals and could one day surpass that of the Communist Party of the Soviet Union.[2] The CCP assumed power in 1949 by means of a civil war victory over the forces of Chiang Kai-shek's Nationalists, who moved the seat of their Republic of China government to the island of Taiwan. The Communists named their new regime the People's Republic of China (PRC). Although the CCP has been continually in power since, China's political institutions and political culture have evolved significantly over those decades, with the CCP's willingness to adapt helping to explain why it has, so far at least, avoided the fate of its sister parties in the Soviet Union and Eastern Europe.

Today, although the Party is committed to maintaining a permanent monopoly on power and is intolerant of those who question its right to rule, analysts consider the political system to be neither monolithic nor rigidly hierarchical. Jockeying among leaders and institutions representing different sets of interests is common at every level of the system. Sometimes fierce competition exists among the members of the Communist Party's nine-man Politburo Standing Committee and 25-member Politburo, China's highest decision-making bodies. It also exists among ministries; between ministries and provincial governments, which are equals in bureaucratic rank; among provinces; and among the service branches of the military. The military and the Foreign Ministry are often on different pages. Even delegates to the National People's Congress, China's weak legislature, sometimes attempt to push back against the government, the courts, and the public prosecutor's office. As part of a trend of very modest political pluralization, moreover, other political actors are increasingly able to influence policy debates. Such actors, who may join forces to advance particular causes, include an increasingly diverse media, state-owned and private corporations, official and quasi-official research institutes, university academics, officially sponsored associations and societies, and grassroots non-governmental organizations.

---

[1] The world's other remaining Communist Party-led states are Cuba, Laos, North Korea, and Vietnam, none of which is a member of the G-20. The G-20 countries are Argentina, Australia, Brazil, Canada, China, France, Germany, India, Indonesia, Italy, Japan, Mexico, Republic of Korea, Russia, Saudi Arabia, South Africa, Turkey, the United Kingdom, and the United States.

[2] China's ruling party is sometimes referred to as the Chinese Communist Party (CCP) and sometimes as the Communist Party of China (CPC). Official Chinese documents most often use the latter formulation. This report uses the former.

One test of a political system is its ability to manage political transitions. At its 18th National Congress later this year, the Party is expected to appoint a new leadership, with Xi Jinping, who is currently the Party's fifth-ranked official, expected to take over the job of Communist Party General Secretary from Hu Jintao, who will be retiring. The Party has worked hard to present the transition as routine and inevitable. It is worth remembering, however, that only the PRC's last two political transitions have been relatively smooth. Those two transitions were from Deng Xiaoping, China's last supreme leader, to a collective leadership led by Party General Secretary Jiang Zemin after Deng's death in 1997, and the transition from Party General Secretary Jiang Zemin to Hu Jintao in 2002. In this transition year, the fall from grace of Communist Party Politburo member and Chongqing Municipality Party Secretary Bo Xilai has already exposed at least one serious rift in the leadership, raised questions about the unity and probity of China's remaining leaders, and, because of Bo's ties to senior military figures, raised questions, too, about the loyalty of parts of the military to the central Party authorities.

Many analysts, both in China and abroad, have questioned the long-term viability of China's current political system, in which the Party remains above the law, leadership politics is a black box, and civil society and the right to free speech and association are severely constrained. China's outgoing Premier Wen Jiabao has called for political reform, including reform of "the leadership system of the party and the state," warning that, "Without the success of political structural reform, it is impossible for us to fully institute economic structural reform. The gains we have made in reform and development may be lost, new problems that have cropped up in China's society cannot be fundamentally resolved and such historical tragedy as the Cultural Revolution may happen again."[3] Wen has not elaborated, though, on precisely what sort of political reform he hopes to see. The views of China's next leaders on the subject remain unknown.

Overview of China's Political Institutions

True to its Leninist roots, the Chinese Communist Party dominates state and society in China. Its power rests on four pillars: its control of China's 2.25 million-strong military, the **People's Liberation Army (PLA)**; its control of personnel appointments across all political institutions, the military, state-owned corporations, and public institutions; its control of the media; and its control of the judiciary and the internal security apparatus. The Party's leadership role is repeatedly referenced in the preamble to the PRC's Constitution, although it is not mentioned in any of the articles of the constitution.[4]

The Party entrusts implementation of its policies and day-to-day administration of the country to the institution of the **State**, headed by the State Council and including the State's ministries and commissions and layers of "people's governments" below the national level. The top State officials at every level of administration usually concurrently hold senior Party posts, to ensure Party control.

---

[3] Ministry of Foreign Affairs of the People's Republic of China, "Premier Wen Jiabao Meets the Press," transcript, March 15, 2012, http://www.fmprc.gov.cn/eng/zxxx/t914983.htm.

[4] The full English-language text of the 1982 state constitution and its subsequent amendments can be accessed on the website of the People's Daily, the mouthpiece of the Communist Party Central Committee, at http://english.peopledaily.com.cn/constitution/constitution.html. Chinese critics of one Party rule sometimes make their case obliquely be calling for revision of the Preamble to the Constitution.

According to China's constitution, the **National People's Congress (NPC)** oversees the State Council, as well as four other institutions: the Presidency, the Supreme People's Court, the public prosecutors' office, and the military. In practice, the NPC, like People's Congresses at every level of administration, is controlled by the Communist Party and is able to exercise little oversight over any of the institutions officially under its supervision. NPC deputies are expected to approve all budgets, agency reports, and personnel appointments put before them. The NPC's most significant power is its ability to initiate and shape legislation.

Although they have little substantive power, the formal political system also includes two other categories of institutions. The first is People's Political Consultative Conferences (PPCCs), the most senior level of which is known as the **Chinese People's Political Consultative Conference (CPPCC) National Committee.** The Party and State ostensibly "consult" with PPCCs on policy issues.[5] The second set of institutions is China's eight **minor political parties,** known as the "democratic parties." All the parties were established before the Communists came to power, pledge loyalty to the Communist Party, and accept its leadership. The existence of the PPCCs and the minor parties allows the Party to describe China's political system as one of "multi-party cooperation and political consultation led by the Communist Party of China."[6]

Features of China's Formal Political Culture

The formal Chinese political system has a number of distinct features. Awareness of these features can be helpful for Congress's interactions with Chinese officials and institutions, and can inform Congress's understanding of official Chinese behavior.

Collective Leadership

China has had no supreme leader since the death of Deng Xiaoping in 1997. The nine men who sit on the country's most senior decision-making body, the Communist Party's Politburo Standing Committee (PSC), form a collective leadership in which each man has a rank, from one to nine, and is responsible for a specific portfolio. Party General Secretary Hu Jintao is ranked first among the nine and has responsibility for convening PSC and larger Politburo meetings. He also controls some of the most consequential portfolios, including military and foreign affairs. Like all his colleagues, however, he must win consensus from the rest of the group for major decisions. Complicating consensus-building is the fact that the members of the PSC owe their jobs to horse trading among different constituencies, interest groups, and influential retired Party elders, whose interests they represent informally on the PSC. PSC decision-making, then, is believed to involve considerable bargaining and maneuvering for factional advantage.[7]

---

[5] The People's Congresses extend down to the township level, one level above the village, and the People's Political Consultative Conferences extend down to the county level, one level above the township.

[6] See discussion of this concept on an authorized Chinese government portal site operated by the CCP's external propaganda arm, the State Council Information Office: http://www.china.org.cn/english/Political/29034.htm.

[7] For more information about the dynamics of the PSC, see Alice L. Miller, "The Politburo Standing Committee under Hu Jintao," *China Leadership Monitor*, no. 35 (September 21, 2011), http://www.hoover.org/publications/china-leadership-monitor/article/93646. The authors are grateful to Prof. Joseph Fewsmith of Boston University for insights into this topic.

The collective leadership feature of the Chinese political system is designed to guard against a repeat of the excesses of the era of the People's Republic of China's founding father, Mao Zedong, when a single out-sized leader was able to convulse the nation with a series of mass political campaigns. It is also meant to guard against the emergence in China of a figure like Mikhail Gorbachev, whose decisions are widely blamed in China for the collapse of the Soviet Union. Nonetheless, the need for consensus accounts in part for the Party's frequently slow public responses to breaking events. In the case of the disgraced former Chongqing Party Secretary, Bo Xilai, the search for consensus may help explain why, after Bo's deputy drew international headlines for seeking refuge at a U.S. diplomatic mission in February 2012, the Party waited nearly six weeks to remove Bo from office in Chongqing, and another nearly four weeks after that to suspend him from his Party positions.

Figure 1. China's National-Level Communist Party Hierarchy

The Politburo Standing Committee is the Most Powerful Decision-Making Body

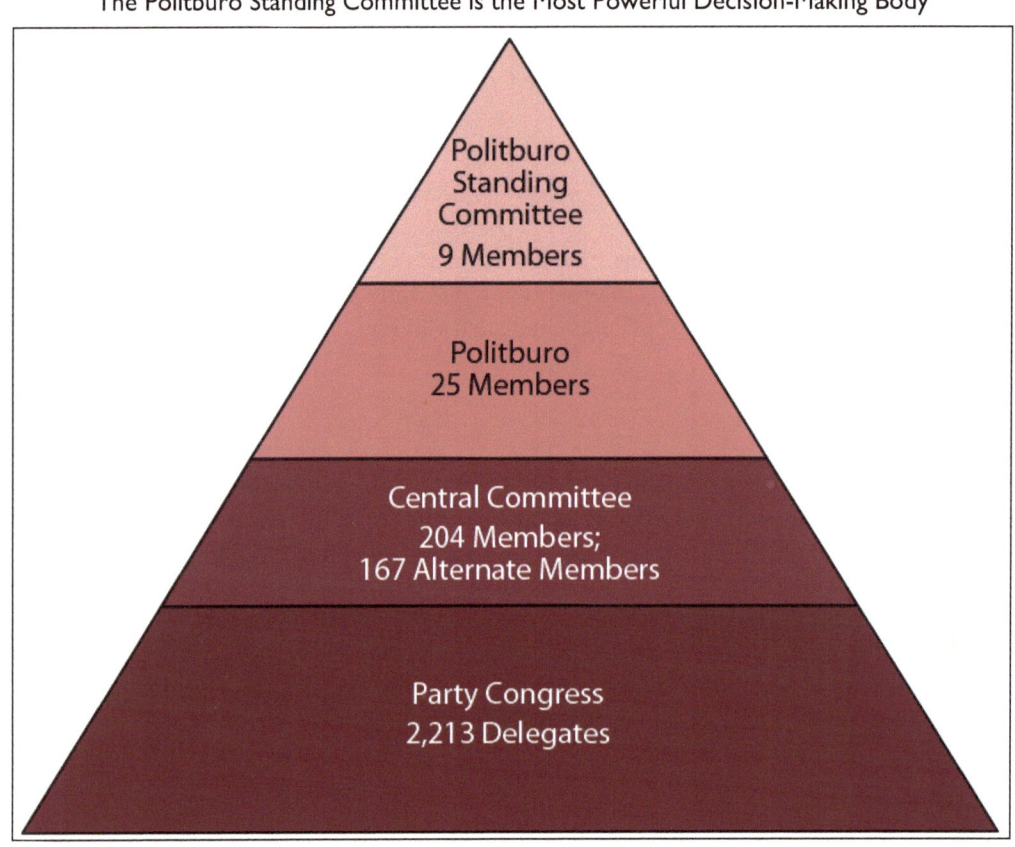

Source: 中共中央组织结构图 (Organizational Structure Chart of the Communist Party Central Committee), http://cpc.people.com.cn/GB/64162/64163/6418742.html.

Note: Numbers of members in each body are accurate as of the start of the current term at the 17th Congress in 2007. With the April 2012 suspension of the former Chongqing Party Secretary, Bo Xilai, from all his Party posts, the Politburo now has 24 members.

The Power of Provincial Governments

Provincial leaders are powerful players in the Chinese political system. Six of them, all Party Secretaries, sit on the Party's Politburo, making them among the two dozen most powerful officials in the country. Provincial leaders also hold two fifths of the seats on the Party's broadest leadership group, the Central Committee, and share at least the same bureaucratic rank as central government ministers. With the 2011 inauguration of a U.S.-China Governors Forum, designed to bring together U.S. governors and Chinese provincial Party secretaries and governors, outreach to provincial leaders has become a new and important element of U.S. policy toward China.

Fiscal decentralization has been a major force empowering provincial governments. Provinces have their own revenue streams, and governments at the provincial level and below are responsible for the lion's share of the country's public expenditure, including almost all public spending on education, health, unemployment insurance, social security, and welfare.[8] Provinces also have the right to pass their own laws and regulations, which may extend national laws and regulations, although not conflict with them. Beijing gives provinces considerable leeway in adopting policies to boost economic growth and encourages provinces to undertake approved policy experiments. In recent years, Guangdong Province, for example, has experimented with easing government control of civil society groups by waiving the long-standing requirement that such groups must have government sponsors in order to register legally.[9]

Beijing sometimes seems to struggle to impose its will on the provinces. Central government ministries have bureaus in the provinces, but they report both to their ministry in Beijing and to the provincial leadership. When priorities conflict, the leaders of such bureaus tend to put the provincial leadership's interests first, if only because the provincial leadership controls their careers. China operates a unitary political system, not a federal system, however, and ultimately, Beijing has the upper hand. Provinces do not have their own constitutions and do not have the power to appoint their own leaders. The Party's Organization Department manages the appointments and promotions of all provincial Party Secretaries and governors, and routinely moves those provincial leaders from province to province, and in and out of posts in Beijing, to ensure that they do not build up regional powerbases. For the same reason, the Party also ensures that military region boundaries do not overlap with provincial boundaries. Beijing's leverage over the provinces includes its ability to send the Party's Central Disciplinary Inspection Commission into provinces to investigate allegations of corruption, and to send the General Auditor's Office into provinces to check their books.[10]

> **Levels of Administration in the PRC**
>
> Central government
>
> Provinces (23); Autonomous Regions (5); Municipalities Under the Central Government (4); and Special Administrative Regions (2)
>
> Municipalities
>
> Counties, County-Level Cities
>
> Townships, Towns

The PRC officially claims 34 provincial-level governments. This includes 23 provinces, five geographic entities that China calls "autonomous regions," which have large ethnic minority populations (Tibet, Xinjiang, Inner Mongolia, Ningxia, and Guangxi); four municipalities that report directly to the central government (Beijing, Shanghai, Tianjin, and Chongqing); and the two special administrative regions of Hong Kong and Macau. (The PRC's count of 23 provinces includes Taiwan, the island of 23 million people that the PRC does not control, but over which it claims sovereignty.) Like ministries and commissions, geographic units can be fiercely competitive among themselves. Their competition can extend to deploying law enforcement, the

---

[8] Tony Saich, *Governance and Politics of China*, 3rd ed. (Palgrave Macmillan, 2011), p. 200.

[9] Wang Jing, "Guangdong Passes a Torch to Civil Society," *Caixin Online*, April 5, 2012, http://english.caixin.com/2012-04-05/100376378.html.

[10] Tony Saich, *Governance and Politics of China*, 3rd ed. (Palgrave Macmillan, 2011), p. 186-187.

courts, and other institutions to support local business interests and throw up barriers to players from other jurisdictions.

Figure 2. Map of China

Showing Provincial-Level Administrative Divisions

Source: Esri Basemaps 2006. Map created by Hannah Fischer, CRS Information Research Specialist.

Notes: (a) Areas shaded in light green are provinces and municipalities that report directly to the central government. Hong Kong and neighboring Macau are Special Administrative Regions. Areas shaded in dark green are autonomous regions with large ethnic minority populations.

(b) The People's Republic of China claims sovereignty over Taiwan and counts it among its provinces, but has never controlled it. Taiwan has been self-governing since 1949.

Document-Based Culture

In the Chinese system, the statements of individual leaders are almost always less authoritative than documents approved by the collective leadership, with the most authoritative documents being those approved by the Communist Party Central Committee. A corollary is that the officially sanctioned published form of a leader's words is almost always more authoritative than the words as originally delivered, with the act of publication providing an important stamp of party approval. Notably, Premier Wen Jiabao, who has a greater level of comfort with extemporaneous speech that any of his colleagues, has used interviews with the foreign media to discuss his ideas for political reform, but the Chinese state media has not reported the substance of those interviews, limiting their authority and impact in China.[11]

China's document-based culture also includes a heavy reliance on paper documents, even in a digital age, with the circulation of paper documents, and the accumulation of signatures on them, helping to build consensus. In the U.S.-China relationship, the great store China places in documents helps explain why the Chinese side has pushed so hard for the issuance of a series of detailed joint statements between the two countries. The Chinese side considers these to be highly authoritative texts containing guiding principles for the relationship, although U.S. officials generally do not accord them similar importance, a disconnect that creates a potentially dangerous expectation gap.

The Importance of Ideology

Ideology matters more in China than in many other political systems. As the Chinese Communist Party has sought to adapt itself to a changing world, it has had to wrestle with ways to revise its ruling ideology to allow the change necessary for its survival, without changing its ideology so much as to undermine further its already tenuous justifications for maintaining a permanent monopoly on power. The CCP waged a successful revolution and established the People's Republic of China with the promise that it would help farmers and workers overthrow their "exploiters," the landlords and capitalists, and establish socialism and ultimately communism, in which all property would be publicly owned, and all classes would cease to exist.[12] In its constitution, the Party still officially proclaims the "realization of communism" to be its "highest ideal and ultimate goal."

As a ruling party, rather than a revolutionary party, however, the CCP now defines itself as representing "the fundamental interests of the overwhelming majority of the Chinese people,"[13] including capitalists. In 2007, long after privately owned businesses began driving double digit economic growth rates in its coastal provinces, and long after its real estate markets began to boom, China finally passed a law protecting private property rights. Each time the Party edges further away from its Marxist roots, even if only to catch up with reality on the ground, it faces howls of protest from China's marginalized but still vocal Marxists. China's preferential treatment of state-owned enterprises (SOEs), a point of friction in U.S.-China relations, is caught up in this ideological debate. The Preamble to CCP's constitution today still holds that, "The Party must uphold and improve the basic economic system, with public ownership playing a dominant role...."[14]

---

[11] For discussion of Wen's calls for political reform, see Alice Miller, "Splits in the Politburo Leadership?," and Joseph Fewsmith, "Political Reform Was Never on the Agenda," *China Leadership Monitor*, no. 34 (February 22, 2011), http://www.hoover.org/publications/china-leadership-monitor/article/67996.

[12] For discussion of the role of ideology in Chinese politics, see William A. Joseph, "Ideology and Chinese Politics," in *Politics in China: An Introduction*, ed. William A. Joseph (Oxford University Press, 2010), pp. 129-164.

[13] Full Text of Constitution of Communist Party of China (as amended on October 21, 2007), http://news.xinhuanet.com/english/2007-10/25/content_6944738.htm.

[14] Ibid.

The Ideal of Meritocracy

An important element of the Communist Party's bid for ideologically-based legitimacy is the notion that people rise within the Party or State hierarchy based on their merit. The Party, which manages personnel appointments across the Chinese political system, the military, and all public institutions, argues that it has a track record of promoting competent administrators, and that this is one of the factors that makes China's political system superior to the political systems of countries that elect their leaders in competitive, multi-party elections. In reality, effectiveness in performing one's duties is just one factor, albeit a significant one, in promotions in China today. Also important are relationships with patrons, which can be built on a shared history of service in a particular place or industrial sector, on shared provincial or school affiliations, or on the basis of family connections. In the case of officials with powerful patrons, less than competent administration is often overlooked.

A serious development that the Party recognizes as threatening its legitimacy has been a rise in the practice of the buying and selling of public office, in which officials illegally auction off political posts to the highest bidders. Meritocracy also breaks down in cases where CCP leaders use their influence to secure positions of authority for their family members, sometimes regardless of their abilities, training, or experience. The children of high-level officials, dubbed "princelings" (*taizi*) in colloquial Chinese, have become a potent force in the Chinese political system. The man expected to become China's next top leader later this year, Xi Jinping, is the son of a revered early revolutionary. So, too, is Bo Xilai, the man ousted from his job as Party Secretary of Chongqing in April 2012 over allegations of corruption.

Age and Term Limits for Official Positions

Although a relatively recent innovation, introduced beginning in 1997, enforcement of age and term limits for top Party and State positions has brought a degree of predictability into otherwise opaque Chinese elite politics. On the basis of the practice at the last two Party Congresses, in 2002 and 2007, analysts expect that officials aged 68 or older will be required to retire from the Politburo and other top Party positions at the 18th Party Congress later this year. Newly appointed members of the Politburo are all expected to be aged 62 or younger. Ministers and provincial Party Secretaries and governors have a retirement age of 65, although those in the middle of their terms are often permitted to serve until age 68.[15] Meanwhile, all top officials are limited to two five-year terms. Those age and term limits define the number of positions that will turn over at each Party Congress and limit the pool of possible candidates. They also benefit officials who have reached senior positions at young ages. The Chinese media have already started to focus attention on officials who were born in the 1960s and now hold the rank of full ministers, with the assumption that they are leading candidates for future top national office.[16]

---

[15] For information about these age restrictions and how top Party officials are selected, see Alice Miller, "The Road to the 18th Party Congress," *China Leadership Monitor*, no. 36 (January 6, 2012), http://www.hoover.org/publications/china-leadership-monitor/article/104231.

[16] See, for example, 尹安学 (Yin Anxue), "专家: "60后'省部级高官增属正常代际变动" ("The Gradual Increase in the Number of 'Post-1960' Province or Minister-Level Senior Officials is Normal Inter-generational Mobility"), *Yangcheng Wanbao* as carried by the *Xinhua News Agency*, April 24, 2011, http://news.xinhuanet.com/politics/2011-04/24/c_121341413.htm. No Party regulation outlining the age limits has been made public. It is unclear whether the post of Central Military Commission chairman is subject to an age limit. Jiang Zemin, who retired from his post as Communist Party Secretary at the 16th Party Congress in 2002, continued to serve as Chairman of the Central Military (continued...)

Emphasis on Long-Term Planning

As a legacy of the centrally planned economic system of the 1950s and 1960s, the Chinese political system places a heavy emphasis on long-term planning. At five-year intervals, the Communist Party General Secretary presents a report to the Party Congress outlining the Party's priorities for the country. It is one of the most authoritative documents in the Chinese political system. China also prepares "Five-Year Plans" that set economic, demographic, and social targets and identify priority industries for development. Other official plans lay out roadmaps for development in various fields over longer time-frames. A roadmap for scientific development, for example, covers the period through 2050.[17] Such plans are not followed to the letter, but they have a powerful role in guiding official policy.

The Communist Party has also tried to apply a long-term planning approach to grooming future political leaders. The most prominent example of an official groomed for high office over a lengthy period is Party General Secretary Hu Jintao, who was appointed to China's top decision-making body as heir apparent to then General Secretary Jiang Zemin in 1992, a full 10 years before he finally ascended to the top job. Xi Jinping, who is expected to be elevated to the post of Party General Secretary later this year, and Li Keqiang, who is expected to become Premier at the NPC's annual session next year, have had shorter, five-year-long apprenticeships.

China's penchant for long-term planning does not always work out in practice. In the post-Mao Zedong era, a Party Chairman has been pushed aside (Hua Guofeng) and two Party General Secretaries purged (Hu Yaobang and Zhao Ziyang), while other senior officials have been felled by politically tinged corruption investigations. With reversals of political fortune, plans have often had to be abandoned.

Emphasis on Political Stability

In 1989, China's Communist Party faced the challenge of large-scale protests in Beijing's Tiananmen Square and in more than a hundred other cities around the country. Disagreements about how to respond split the top Party leadership and forced out the Party General Secretary at the time. The decision by Deng Xiaoping, then China's supreme leader, to order in the army to clear the Beijing protesters by force undermined the Party's legitimacy and severely damaged China's standing in the world. Since then, the Party has made maintenance of social stability one of its top priorities, deploying a vast internal security apparatus to head off protests or, once they erupt, to prevent them from spreading.

The domestic security apparatus includes an 800,000-strong police force, under the Ministry of Public Security, and a 1.5 million-strong paramilitary force, the People's Armed Police, which reports to both the Party's Central Military Commission and, through the Ministry of Public Security, to the State Council. The 2.25 million-strong People's Liberation Army also has a domestic stability mandate, on top of its national defense mandate. Other agencies involved in internal security include the Party's Propaganda Department, which plays an important role in

---

(...continued)

Commission for another two years, until 2004, when he was 78.

[17] The science plan, issued by the Chinese Academy of Sciences in 2009, is entitled, "Innovation 2050: The Science and Technology Revolution and China's Future" (创新2050: 科技革命于中国的未来).

censoring the media to prevent discussion of subjects that might feed movements for change; the Ministry of State Security, which focuses on internal security threats as well as conducting intelligence-gathering abroad; and the Ministry of Justice, which operates China's prison system.[18] All but the Propaganda Department are overseen by the Party's Central Commission of Politics and Law and all are powerful bureaucratic players in the Chinese political system. Since 2010, China's spending on such internal security agencies as the police, the People's Armed Police, the courts, and the prison system has outstripped its spending on the military. The 2012 national budget contained planned spending of $111.4 billion on internal security (not including the PLA), compared to $106.4 billion on defense.[19]

Governance Challenges in the Chinese Political System

Since 1978, the CCP has worked to build, almost entirely from scratch, a set of governing institutions and a system of laws capable of handling rapid economic and social development at home and ever more complex interactions with the global community. The Communist Party's insistence on the principle of unchallenged Communist Party rule atop this system has been one of the few constants in the process. Sweeping re-organizations of government have been common, with the establishment of new agencies and coordinating committees, the spinning off of the old "line" ministries, mergers of other ministries, and adjustments to the bureaucratic status and/or jurisdiction of many government bodies. Keeping track of the changes adds to the challenge of understanding China's policy process. These institutional reforms have not, however, managed to solve some enduring challenges in the Chinese system undermining effective governance.

"Stove-Piping" and Bureaucratic Competition

Among the Chinese political system's governance difficulties is the phenomenon known as "stove-piping," in which individual ministries and other hierarchies share information up and down the chain of command, but not horizontally with each other. China has no coordinating body analogous to the U.S. National Security Council. "Leading Small Groups" at the top of the Party and the State seek to bring together representatives from multiple agencies to coordinate and build consensus around policy in specific areas, but they have small staffs, vary widely in their level of activity, and are usually unwilling to get involved in forcing day-to-day coordination among their member agencies. In the U.S.-China relationship, one of the values U.S. officials see in the Strategic & Economic Dialogue (S&ED) mechanism is that it forces multiple Chinese agencies to come together under one roof to talk with the U.S. government about issues in the relationship, and, as a side benefit, to talk to each other.

A related governance issue is unproductive competition among official entities. It is not uncommon in China for multiple entities to attempt to assert jurisdiction over the same issue, competing with each other for scarce budget resources, power, and recognition from higher

---

[18] For an overview of the internal security apparatus, see Richard D. Fisher, Jr., *China's Military Modernization: Building for Regional and Global Reach* (Stanford University Press, 2010), pp. 32-34.

[19] "China Domestic Security Spending Rises to $111 billion," *Reuters*, March 5, 2012.

government officials. A recent report by the International Crisis Group, a Brussels-based non-governmental organization, identified no fewer than 11 ministerial-level official entities, including three provincial governments, plus five law enforcement agencies under their control, all jostling to assert themselves in the South China Sea, with no effective national-level mechanism to coordinate their activities. The report blamed their "conflicting mandates and lack of coordination" for stoking tensions in the region.[20] Alternatively, bureaucratic competition can sometimes result in agencies declining to implement each other's policies, with the claim that they lack budget resources or manpower.

The Distorting Influence of Bureaucratic Rank

Chinese political culture features carefully observed systems of ranks that identify the relative importance of people, official agencies, public institutions, state-owned corporations, and geographic units. Rank consciousness affects the way that officials and their agencies interact with each other. Most damagingly, it contributes to the political system's difficulty in achieving successful inter-agency coordination and frequently undermines lines of authority.

Among the rules that govern rank in China is that entities of equivalent rank cannot issue binding orders to each other. Often, they cannot even compel coordination, although Party entities and security agencies have more clout in that respect than other entities. An entity of lesser rank seeking to coordinate with an entity of higher rank faces a daunting challenge. Many analysts attribute the well documented communication problems between the People's Liberation Army (PLA) and the Foreign Ministry to the large gap in their respective ranks. The PLA's Central Military Commission is of equivalent rank to the State Council, China's cabinet, while the Foreign Ministry is a mere ministry under the State Council. For the Foreign Ministry to liaise with the PLA, it must report up to the State Council, which may have to report up further up to the Politburo in order to secure PLA cooperation.[21]

In another example of the distorting influence of rank, state-owned enterprises sometimes outrank the Party and state leaders in the geographic jurisdictions in which they are based, making it impossible for the local government to issue binding orders to them.[22] The rank system can also impede effective regulatory oversight when regulators share the same bureaucratic rank as entities they are charged with regulating. For example, while China's banking regulator, the China Banking Regulatory Commission (CBRC), has ministerial rank, and China's five largest banks have quasi ministerial rank, at the province-level they have equal rank, resulting in resistance from the banks' provincial branches to the provincial CBRC's oversight.[23] A recent hot topic in

---

[20] International Crisis Group, *Stirring Up the South China Sea*, Asia Report No. 223, April 23, 2012, pp. 8-13, http://www.crisisgroup.org/~/media/Files/asia/north-east-asia/223-stirring-up-the-south-china-sea-i.pdf.

[21] Carnegie Endowment for International Peace scholar Michael Swaine reports that within the PLA, rank differences can impede coordination between the units in charge of operations and training, which are more senior in the PLA hierarchy, and those in charge of foreign affairs and intelligence, which are more junior, even when training exercises have foreign policy implications. Michael D. Swaine, "China's Assertive Behavior Part Three: The Role of the Military in Foreign Policy," *China Leadership Monitor*, no. 36 (January 6, 2012), p. 9, http://www.hoover.org/publications/china-leadership-monitor/article/104181.

[22] The Brookings Institution's Kenneth Lieberthal makes this point as part of an insightful discussion of the role of rank in the Chinese political system in Kenneth Lieberthal, *Managing the China Challenge: How to Achieve Corporate Success in the People's Republic* (Brookings Institution Press, 2011), pp. 50-52.

[23] "全国金融工作会议将讨论改革金融企业行政级别" ("National Financial Work Meeting Will Discuss Reform of Administrative Ranks for Financial Institutions"), 21世纪经济报道 *(21ˢᵗ Century Business Herald)*, December 5, 2006. (continued...)

Chinese policy circles has been a proposal to create an Energy Ministry. Those who favor an Energy Ministry argue that it is needed because some of China's major energy firms, including such global oil industry giants as Sinopec and CNPC, have ministerial rank, and thus outrank the agency currently tasked with overseeing the energy sector, the National Energy Administration, which has only quasi ministerial status.[24]

One solution periodically proposed for some of these rank-related governance issues is simply to abolish administrative ranks for the leaders of state-owned enterprises and financial institutions. So far, however, such reforms have not taken hold. One reason may be the unwillingness of corporate bosses to give up the array of privileges that accompany administrative rank. According to a recent article in China's respected Southern Weekend newspaper, those with the rank of full ministers are assigned a car costing up to $71,000, with a full-time driver; provided state funds for the purchase of residences up to 2,400 square feet in size; and given access to exclusive health care, including single-person VIP hospital rooms and the convenience of having all medical bills automatically settled by the Ministry of Health. All those privileges continue for life, with health privileges being the most prized. Retired full minister-rank officials are also assigned a full-time secretary, again for life.[25]

A long-time challenge for the U.S.-China relationship has been that China considers U.S. cabinet secretaries to be of equivalent rank to Chinese ministers, rather than to China's more senior vice premiers and state councilors. The creation of the U.S.-China Strategic and Economic Dialogue (S&ED) allowed the United States to bypass the rank system and find a way for the U.S. Secretaries of the Treasury and State to deal directly with their real counter-parts above the ministerial level. The U.S. Secretary of Defense, however, is still hosted by the Chinese Minister of Defense, who has less authority than all 11 of his colleagues on the Central Military Commission and is outside the operational chain of command.

(...continued)

http://finance.people.com.cn/GB/1040/5124620.html. The five banks in question are ICBC, Agricultural Bank of China, Bank of China, China Construction Bank, and Bank of Communications.

[24] Yang Shisheng and Lin Xiao, "改革下一步: 成立能源部" ("The Next Step in Reform: Establishing a Ministry of Energy"), 华夏时报*(Huaxia Shibao/China Times)*, April 20, 2012, http://www.chinatimes.cc/yaowen/hongguan/2012-04-20/30139.shtml.

[25] Qian Haoping, "中国有多少部级单位?" ("How Many "Ministerial-Level" Units Does China Have?"), 南方周末 *(Southern Weekend)*, February 16, 2012.

Table 1. Select Chinese Institutions and Their Bureaucratic Ranks

Rank	Institutions
Full State （正国级）	Communist Party Central Committee; Party and State Central Military Commissions; The State Council; National People's Congress Standing Committee; Chinese People's Political Consultative Conference National Committee; State Presidency
Quasi State （副国级）	Communist Party Central Disciplinary Inspection Commission (the Party's graft-fighting arm); Supreme People's Court; Supreme People's Procuratorate (the public prosecutor's office)
Ministry/Province （正部省级)	Party departments (e.g. Party Organization Department, Party Propaganda Department); ministries, commissions, and general administrations; regulatory commissions (e.g., for banking, insurance and securities); provinces and autonomous regions; municipalities under the central government (Beijing, Shanghai, Tianjin, and Chongqing); Hong Kong and Macau; some large state enterprises (e.g., Sinopec); "mass organizations" such as the Communist Youth League and the All-China Federation of Trade Unions; the Xinhua News Agency; research academies (the Chinese Academy of Social Sciences, the Chinese Academy of Sciences, and the Chinese Academy of Engineering)
Quasi Ministry/Province Rank (副部省级)	State bureaus, offices, and administrations (e.g., State Statistical Bureau, State Intellectual Property Office, State Oceanic Administration, State Food and Drug Administration); 15 cities (Changchun, Chengdu, Dalian, Hangzhou, Harbin, Guangzhou, Ji'nan, Nanjing, Ningbo, Qingdao, Shenyang, Shenzhen, Wuhan, Xiamen, and Xi'an); China's five largest banks; some large state enterprises (e.g., the China National Tobacco Corporation); 32 universities

Source: Chinese media reports.

Weak Rule of Law and Ineffective Policy Implementation and Enforcement

A long-standing source of frustration for U.S. government officials working with Chinese counterparts is their seeming inability or unwillingness to enforce policies, laws, and regulations, much less the state constitution. Scholars of China have identified many factors that contribute to this situation. One issue is the role of the Party. Although it has offered strong rhetorical support for the rule of law, the Party has continued to insist on its members being held above the law. In the case of a Party official accused of wrongdoing, such as the former Chongqing Party Secretary Bo Xilai, the Party conducts its own investigation and then chooses whether to hand the accused over to the state judicial authorities.[26] Judicial authorities cannot investigate without the Party's consent. The Party also explicitly denies the judiciary independence, insisting that Party Commissions of Politics and Law oversee the work of the police, the prosecutor's office, and the courts. The commissions are empowered to intervene to obtain outcomes in the Party's interest, further undermining the authority of the law.

Other issues include the rank system, bureaucratic competition, and the relative power of provincial leaders, as discussed above. (See "The Power of Provincial Governments.") Because central government ministries and provincial governments are of equal rank, ministries have trouble forcing provinces to implement policies that provincial authorities may see as compromising their interests, particularly in an area such as environmental protection, and particularly when a mandate is unfunded, as central government mandates frequently are. Similarly, the bureaucratic status of the courts is such that they often cannot compel other agencies, much less other jurisdictions, to enforce their judgments.[27]

Yet another factor affecting enforcement of policies, laws, and regulations is judgments about their relative authority. China's most authoritative laws are "basic laws" and other laws passed by the NPC in full session. Laws passed by the NPC's Standing Committee are slightly less authoritative. Less authoritative still are State Council regulations, and then ministerial

> ## Liu Xia, Chen Guangcheng, and the Rule of Law
>
> Chinese authorities tend to be particularly cavalier about the rule of law in the cases where they perceive a political threat. Although she has been accused of no crimes, Liu Xia, the wife of imprisoned dissident Liu Xiaobo, has been under an extra-judicial form of house arrest since the announcement of her husband's Nobel Peace Prize in 2010. Chen Guangcheng, a blind legal advocate who exposed coercive birth control policies in his home province of Shandong, was sentenced to four years in prison on charges that including disrupting traffic, and then placed under extra-judicial house arrest in his home village after the completion of his sentence in 2010. In April 2012, he escaped his captors and sought refuge in the U.S. Embassy in Beijing for six days while U.S. and Chinese government officials negotiated over his fate. In a video posted online and in media interviews since leaving the Embassy, he has challenged the central government over its failure to intervene with the Shandong Provincial authorities to end his illegal confinement, despite extensive foreign media coverage of his circumstances and pressure from foreign governments. He is now awaiting Chinese processing of a passport that would allow him to travel to the United States.

---

[26] So far, Bo is still in the Party system. His wife, who is alleged to be implicated in a murder, has been turned over to judicial authorities, prompting speculation that she may not be a Party member.

[27] According to Harvard University professor Tony Saich, "The legal system is simply one specific cog in a bureaucratic machine that is built to achieve state objectives. It enjoys parity with other bureaucratic entities and thus there is no immediate notion that the decision of a court is binding on another administrative agency or across different geographical locations." Tony Saich, *Governance and Politics of China*, 3rd ed. (New York: Palgrave Macmillan, 2011), pp. 162-163.

regulations. Policy documents have their own pecking order. Officials tasked with implementation and enforcement are keenly aware of the distinctions, and tailor their enforcement activities accordingly. Finally, enforcement can be undermined by the need to wait for implementing regulations, which can take years to produce, if they are produced at all. Civil society groups have long lobbied for a greater role in monitoring enforcement, but the CCP continues to resist, fearing empowering groups outside its control.

Factionalism

Although China is effectively a one party state, multiple coalitions, factions, and constituencies exist within the political system. Political mentorship, place of birth, the affiliations of one's parents, and common educational or work history may lead individuals to form political alliances. Former Party General Secretary Jiang Zemin, for example, was known for promoting and relying upon a group of officials he had known from his days as Mayor and then Party Secretary of Shanghai, who also shared his interest in fast-paced economic growth and breaking down ideological barriers to the growth of the private sector. Party General Secretary Hu Jintao, for his part, has promoted a number of officials who, like him, worked for the Communist Youth League, and who support his push to address income inequality. Some analysts speculate that China's likely next top leader, Xi Jinping, may favor fellow "princelings," officials whose fathers or fathers-in-law were senior Party officials, although, as the Bo Xilai affair demonstrated, princelings do not share a single political outlook. Increasingly, scholars see competition within the party and the state based on bureaucratic constituencies, too. The Ministry of Industry and Information Technology backs industry, for example, against the Ministry of Environment, which seeks to rein in industrial pollution. Two of the nine members of the current Politburo Standing Committee have backgrounds in the oil industry, and may be inclined to support the oil industry's interests in policy discussions.

Corruption

Corruption in China is widespread and takes many forms, from lavish gifts and expensive meals bestowed on officials by those seeking favors, to bribes explicitly offered in exchange for permits and approvals, to embezzlement of state funds, exemption of friends and relatives from enforcement of laws and regulations, and the appointment of relatives to lucrative jobs in state-owned companies. A 2011 report released by China's Central Bank estimated that from the mid-1990s to 2008, corrupt officials who fled overseas took with them $120 billion in stolen funds.[28] The CCP uses its Central Discipline Inspection Commission (CDIC) to police its own ranks for corruption, an arrangement fraught with conflicts of interest. As noted above, the Party metes out its own punishments for wrongdoing by its members, and has sole discretion about whether to hand members over to the state judiciary for investigation and possible prosecution. (See "Weak Rule of Law and Ineffective Policy Implementation and Enforcement.") Critics charge that CDIC investigations are frequently politically motivated, even if they uncover real wrongdoing. Officials who keep on the right side of their superiors and colleagues may engage in large-scale corruption, while other officials may be investigated for lesser infractions because they have fallen afoul of powerful officials.

---

[28] "Chinese Officials Stole $120 billion, Fled Mainly to US," *BBC News*, June 17, 2011.

The Bo Xilai Affair

On April 10, 2012, the Communist Party suspended one of its top leaders, Bo Xilai, from his posts on the Party's Politburo and Central Committee, and announced that the Party's graft-fighting arm, the Central Discipline Inspection Commission, would be investigating him for alleged "serious discipline violations." The Party had removed Bo from his post as Party Secretary of powerful Chongqing Municipality nearly a month earlier. Also on April 10, China's official Xinhua News Agency announced that Bo's wife, Gu Kailai, had been handed over to state judicial authorities on suspicion of involvement in the November 2011 murder in Chongqing of a British businessman. The authorities indicated that the investigation into the alleged murder was spurred by information provided by Bo's former police chief and vice mayor in Chongqing, Wang Lijun, who sparked headlines around the world when he sought refuge in the U.S. Consulate in Chengdu for approximately 30 hours on February 6 and 7, 2012, and then gave himself up to Chinese security officials.

With the Communist Party scheduled to undertake a sweeping generational leadership transition at the 18th Party Congress later this year, Bo's ouster has up-ended the Party's effort to present the transition as smooth and uneventful. Bo's fall has raised questions about the unity of the Party's remaining top leadership and the loyalty of segments of the military to the Party. As details of the Bo family's wealth emerge, it has also highlighted the degree to which the families of top Party officials have been able to parlay access to political power into vast personal wealth, information that may further harm the Party's already fragile legitimacy. Finally, with the role micro-bloggers have played in moving events in the Bo saga forward, the Bo affair has highlighted the challenge the Communist Party faces in controlling information and narratives in a social media age.

Bo's former police chief appears to have sealed Bo's fate when he took his allegations against his boss to U.S. diplomats, thus ensuring that the allegations could not be contained. Until then, Bo appeared to be riding high. Media-savvy and relishing the limelight, he had drawn national attention by styling himself as a champion of the poor and dispossessed, throwing his support behind the state-owned economy, leading a brutal crackdown on alleged organized crime bosses, and fanning nostalgia for the more egalitarian ethos of the Mao Zedong era, including by encouraging the mass singing of "red" songs from the chaotic and violent Cultural Revolution movement of the 1960s and 1970s. Bo's egalitarian rhetoric was implicitly critical of Party General Secretary Hu Jintao and Premier Wen Jiabao's failure to narrow one of the world's starkest wealth gaps. His supporters included those uncomfortable with the ideological compromises and broken promises to the working class that have accompanied China's rise to become the world's second largest economy. Riding his notoriety, Bo was widely reported to be angling for promotion to the Party's top decision-making body, the nine-member Politburo Standing Committee, later this year.

Having come together, after weeks of indecision, to remove Bo from office, the collective Party leadership now faces the challenge of convincing Bo's supporters that the allegations against Bo and his wife are genuine, and not a pretext for disposing of a political and ideological challenger. The leadership also faces the challenge of convincing the Party rank and file, Chinese society, and the world that they are united, and that the Bo affair has not sown serious divisions among them. One of the key lessons that the Party drew from the events of the spring of 1989 was that splits in the leadership embolden those with grievances against the Party, and that events can quickly spin out of control.

China's Political Institutions in Detail

The Chinese Communist Party (CCP)

The Communist Party's 80 million members constitute approximately 6% of China's population of 1.34 billion. Any Chinese citizen over the age of 18 who is willing to accept and abide by the Party's constitution and policies, which include a requirement that Party members be atheists, can apply for Party membership. In 2010, however, of 21 million applicants, just under 15% were accepted. The Party is heavily male, with female members making up less than a quarter of the total.[29] Party membership is considered prestigious, although not to the degree that it was in earlier eras.

Every Party member, irrespective of position, must be organized into a branch, cell, or other specific unit of the Party to participate in the regular activities of the Party organization. Party units exist in all official and semi-official organizations and institutions, including state-owned enterprises and universities. As of 2010, they also existed in more than 400,000 private businesses and foreign-owned enterprises, and the party has sought to establish them in social organizations, too.[30] These Party bodies can wield great power within an institution, even though in some cases, as in foreign-owned companies, they may have little formal authority. With the Party controlling all avenues for public sector advancement, it is thought that many young people join the Party for career reasons.

Party policy is communicated down the layers of the Party organization by means of directives and Party committee meetings. At these meetings, Party members review and discuss the directives. The Party also ensures ideological conformity through nationwide study campaigns. In September 2008, for example, the Party launched an 18-month-long campaign for Party members to study Communist Party General Secretary Hu Jintao's concept of "scientific development." Party members throughout the system were required to study speeches and documents related to the concept. Party publishing houses published study guides. In another example, in 2009, as part of a broader study campaign on "the theory of socialism with Chinese characteristics," the Party's Propaganda Department ordered Party organizations nationwide to lead study sessions on a set of concepts known as the "Six Why's." Among the six why's were why separation of powers and a Western-style multi-party system were not right for China.[31]

At the top of the Party's hierarchy, the most powerful policy- and decision-making entity is the **Politburo Standing Committee (PSC),** currently comprised of nine officials. They are all members of the broader **Politburo**, which started its current term with a membership of 25. Politburo members are all members of broadest senior grouping of Communist Party officials, the **Central Committee,** which has approximately 370 full and alternate members. (See **Figure 1** for an illustration of the Party hierarchy.)

As noted above, each member of the PSC has a rank, from one to nine, and is responsible for a specific portfolio. (See "Collective Leadership.") To ensure Party control, the top-ranked members of the PSC serve concurrently as the heads of other parts of the political system. The top ranked PSC member, Party General Secretary Hu Jintao, for example, serves concurrently as head of the military, in his capacity as head of Chairman of the **Central Military Commission**, and as the head of State, in his capacity as State President. The second-ranked PSC member, Wu Bangguo, serves as Chairman of the National People's Congress (NPC), while the third-ranked PSC member, Wen Jiabao, serves as Premier of the State Council, and the fourth-ranked member,

---

[29] Zhao Lei, "More than 80 million are Party members," *China Daily*, June 25, 2011. The article cites statistics released by the Organization Department of the Communist Party Central Committee.

[30] According to the Party's webpage, "Primary Party organizations are formed in China's mainland enterprises, rural areas, government departments, schools, scientific research institutes, communities, mass organizations, intermediaries, companies of the People's Liberation Army and other basic units, where there are at least three full Party members." In 2010, according to a Party spokesman, 22% of enterprises had Party organizations within them, including 438,000 "non-public" enterprises. Xinhua, "China's Communist Party Members near 78M," *The China Daily*, June 28, 2010.

[31] Theory Bureau, CCP Central Committee Propaganda Department, *Six "Why's": Answers to Some Important Questions (六个 为什么': 对几个重大问题的回答)* (Study Press 学习出版社 2009).

Jia Qinglin, heads the Chinese People's Political Consultative Conference (CPPCC) and oversees the Party's relations with non-Communist groups. Portfolios for other PSC members include the propaganda system; management of the Party bureaucracy and Hong Kong and Macau; finance and economics; Party discipline; and the internal security system.[32]

PSC members also head Party **"Leading Small Groups" (LSGs)** for their policy areas. LSGs are secretive bodies intended to facilitate cross-agency coordination in implementation of Politburo Standing Committee decisions. The National Security Leading Small Group and the Foreign Affairs Leading Small Group, for example, are both headed by Party General Secretary Hu Jintao.

The next highest decision-making body is the full **Politburo**, which, with the suspension of the disgraced former Chongqing Party Secretary, Bo Xilai, now comprises 24 officials. In addition to the nine members of the PSC, Politburo members include the heads of major departments of the Party bureaucracy, the two highest ranking officers in the Chinese military, State Council Vice Premiers, a State Councilor, and Party leaders from important cities and provinces. The current Politburo has only one female member. Because of its relatively unwieldy size and the geographic diversity of its members, the full Politburo is not involved in day-to-day decision-making. In 2011, it met eight times, with its meetings often focused on a single major policy area or on preparations for major national meetings.[33]

According to the Party's constitution, the PSC and Politburo derive their power from the **Central Committee**, whose full and alternate members together "elect" the Politburo, Politburo Standing Committee, and Party General Secretary, and "decide" on the composition of the Party's Central Military Commission.[34] In practice, incumbent top officials provide a list of nominees to the Central Committee, which ratifies the leadership's nominees.[35] The current nearly 400-member Central Committee (including alternates) is made up of leaders from the provinces (41.5%), central ministries (22.6%), the military (17.5 %), central Party organizations (5.9%), and state-owned enterprises, educational institutions, "mass organizations" such as the Communist Youth League, and other constituencies (12.4%).[36]

---

[32] Alice L. Miller, "The Politburo Standing Committee under Hu Jintao," *China Leadership Monitor*, no. 35 (September 21, 2011), http://www.hoover.org/publications/china-leadership-monitor/article/93646. For a discussion of the history of Leading Small Groups and their current role, see Alice L. Miller, "The CCP Central Committee's Leading Small Groups," *China Leadership Monitor,* no. 26 (September 2, 2008), http://www.hoover.org/publications/china-leadership-monitor/article/5689.

[33] The website of the Party Central Committee's mouthpiece, the People's Daily, contains a list of Politburo meetings and their agendas going back to 2002. See http://cpc.people.com.cn/GB/64162/106114/214622/index.html.

[34] The Party's constitution, which was most recently revised in 2007, is available in English at http://news.xinhuanet.com/english/2007-10/25/content_6944738.htm and in Chinese at http://news.xinhuanet.com/ziliao/2002-11/18/content_633225.htm.

[35] In 2007, the process for development of the nominees list was modestly more inclusive a process than previously. The Party leadership drew up a list of nearly 200 candidates for nominations and then invited all full and alternate members of the Central Committee and other unidentified Party figures to vote upon them. The Party leadership reportedly drew upon the results of this straw poll in developing its final list of 25 Politburo nominees for Central Committee ratification, although it was not bound by the straw poll's results. Alice Miller, "The Road to the 18th Party Congress," *China Leadership Monitor*, no. 36 (January 6, 2012), p. 9, http://www.hoover.org/publications/china-leadership-monitor/article/104231.

[36] Cheng Li, "A Pivotal Stepping-Stone: Local Leaders' Representation on the 17th Central Committee," *China Leadership Monitor*, no. 23 (January 23, 2008), p. 1, http://www.hoover.org/publications/china-leadership-monitor/article/5772.

The Central Committee, in turn, is elected by the approximately 2,000 delegates to **Party National Congresses**, which are held every five years. Congress delegates also approve the Party General Secretary's report to the Congress, which serves as a statement of the Party's positions and an outline of the Party's agenda for the coming five years. The Party's 18th Congress is scheduled for later this year and will anoint a new generation of national leaders.

In the years between Party Congresses, the Central Committee is required to meet at least once a year, with each meeting known as a ***plenum*** (or *plenary session*). Plenums usually focus on setting the direction for the country in a specific area, while also approving major personnel decisions. In October 2010, for example, the Fifth Plenum of the 17th Central Committee discussed and approved a draft of the 12th Five-Year Plan for China's economy, covering the years 2011 to 2015. It also approved the appointment of Xi Jinping to be first vice chairman of the CMC, a move widely seen as the last step in Xi's preparation to become the top ranked official in the Communist Party in 2012. At the end of each plenum, the Party issues a public document, known as a ***communiqué***, announcing the major decisions taken.

Under the Central Committee and the Party Secretariat, the CCP operates an expansive bureaucracy that reaches into many aspects of government and society, and parts of which extend deep down into local governments. One powerful part of that bureaucracy is the **Organization Department**, which is responsible for training officials and assigning them to positions across the party and state, the legislatures, state-owned corporations; universities; and other public institutions. Another is the **Propaganda (or "Publicity") Department**, responsible for the Party's messaging and for control of the media. The **Central Commission of Politics and Law** ensures Party control over the internal security apparatus. The **United Front Work Department** is responsible for relations with the people of Taiwan, Hong Kong, and Macau, non-Communist groups, and ethnic minorities and Chinese living outside mainland China. The Party's **International Department** handles relations with foreign political parties. It is a particularly influential player in China's relationships with fellow socialist countries, including North Korea. Sub-national offices of the Party's bureaucracy report both to the head of the local Party Committee, who holds the title of Party Secretary, and to the higher-level Party bureaucracy.

The People's Liberation Army (PLA)

The People's Liberation Army, or PLA, is China's military. Officially, the PLA reports to both a **Party Central Military Commission (CMC)** and a **State CMC**. Both are currently headed by Hu Jintao in his capacity as the Communist Party General Secretary and State President and have identical memberships. They are effectively a single body, with the Party CMC the real locus of authority. The PLA is a Party army, rather than a national army, meaning that the PLA is expected to put the Party's interests ahead of those of the nation. The Party has emphasized this point repeatedly in the aftermath of the fall of the former Chongqing Party chief Bo Xilai, who is believed to have had powerful allies in the military.

The PLA's role in politics has been much debated. One leading U.S. expert describes the Party as having made "a deliberate decision to remove the military from elite politics and the most powerful decision-making councils, and to regularize and institutionalize its role in the policy process as a professional force." As evidence of that trend, he cites statistics on uniformed military representation on top Party bodies. The Communist Party's top decision-making body, the PSC, has had no uniformed military representation since 1997. Uniformed military officers hold just two of the current 24 spots on the Politburo, although nearly 20% of Central Committee members have military affiliations. Yet the military has a direct line to the Communist Party

General Secretary, the top official in the Chinese political system, through the Central Military Commission. Senior military officers also sit on Party "Leading Small Groups" on such issues as foreign affairs, national security, and Taiwan affairs.[37]

Individual members of the military have emerged in recent years as influential media commentators, particularly on foreign policy, although it is not clear how authoritative their statements are. One such high-profile commentator is Major General Luo Yuan. His rank would seem to lend him authority, but his institutional affiliation, as executive board member of a research society under the PLA's Academy of Military Sciences, would seem to put him at some remove from any operational decisions.[38]

A major tool for Party control of the military is the General Political Department (GPD), one of four "general departments" of the military represented on the CMC. Among other things, the GPD is responsible for political training, military media and cultural activities, and military personnel matters, including management of personnel dossiers, promotions, and job assignments. GPD political commissars (known at lower levels as political directors and political instructors) serve side-by-side with military commanders at all levels of the PLA, and head the Party committees in all PLA units. Almost all PLA officers are Party members.[39]

The PLA's other general departments are the General Staff Department (GSD), responsible for operations, intelligence, professional education, and foreign affairs; the General Logistics Department (GLD), which handles military pay, supplies, healthcare, and transportation; and the General Armaments Department (GAD), which manages the PLA's weapons and equipment needs and also oversees China's manned space program.[40]

The CMC uses the four general departments, which are dominated by the ground forces, to direct three military service branches, plus China's strategic missile forces, the Second Artillery Force, and seven military regions, also known as military area commands or theaters of war. A paramilitary force, the People's Armed Police, which plays a major role in putting down domestic unrest, reports to both the Central Military Commission and the State's leading body, the State Council, through the Ministry of Public Security. It is ultimately overseen, however, by the Party's Central Commission of Politics and Law.

---

[37] Michael D. Swaine, "China's Assertive Behavior Part Three: The Role of the Military in Foreign Policy," *China Leadership Monitor*, no. 36 (January 6, 2012), pp. 3-6, http://www.hoover.org/publications/china-leadership-monitor/article/104181.

[38] For a profile of Luo Yuan, see Ed Zhang, "General Luo Yuan, the Cool-Headed Hardliner," *South China Morning Post*, March 16, 2012.

[39] Dennis J. Blasko, *The Chinese Army Today: Tradition and Transformation for the 21st Century*, 2nd ed. (New York: Routledge, 2012), pp. 33-34.

[40] Dennis J. Blasko, *The Chinese Army Today: Tradition and Transformation for the 21st Century*, 2nd ed. (New York: Routledge, 2012), pp. 33-35.

Figure 3. Organization Chart for the People's Liberation Army

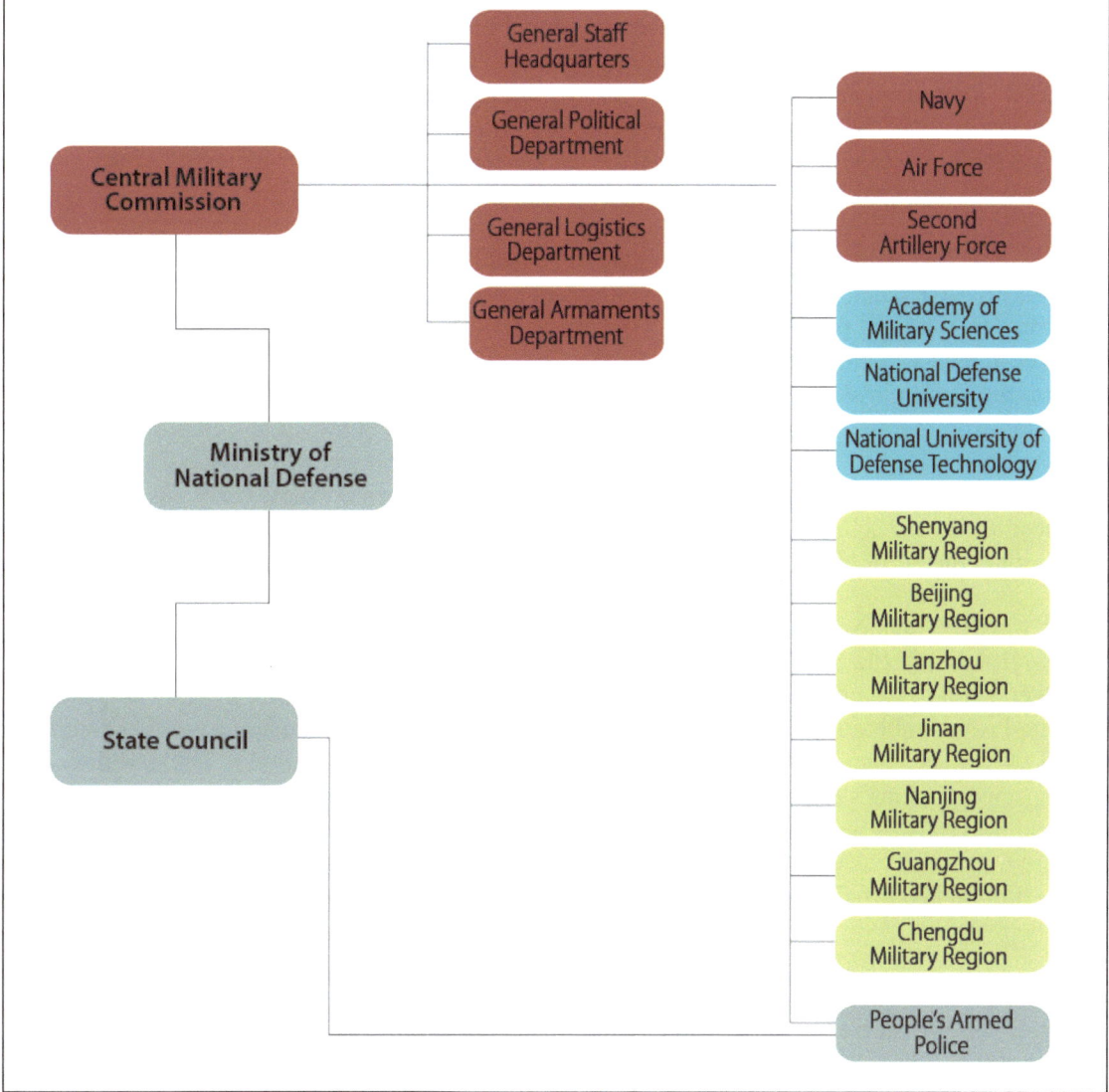

Source: Dennis J. Blasko, *The Chinese Army Today: Tradition and Transformation for the 21st Century*, 2nd ed. (New York: Routledge, 2012), p. 32. Color shading added by CRS.

Notes: Entities in red are represented on the Central Military Commission. The People's Armed Police reports to both the Central Military Commission and, through the Ministry of Public Security, to the State Council.

The State

The second major institution of the Chinese political structure is the State. During the early decades of Communist rule, the Party and the State operated as one under a slogan trumpeting "the Party's absolute and unified leadership." In the late 1970s, however, the Communist Party began moves to separate Party and government functions, authorizing a cabinet, the State Council, and "people's governments" at lower levels to manage the day-to-day administration of the country.[41] To ensure its control over the State system, the Party still maintains a robust presence inside the system. The top officials at each level of the State system routinely hold concurrent Party posts, although they often do not publicize them, and Party committees are embedded in the State Council, ministries, and government departments at every level. While powerful Communist Party bodies that exist in parallel to the State bodies set the policy direction for the country at all levels and make major decisions, the State system implements and executes policy. In recent decades, State leaders have been particularly focused on managing China's economy, leaving "political" matters, such as ideology and personnel, to the Party.

The personnel working for the government are civil servants. While most senior government officials are CCP members, party membership is not a requirement for higher government positions. In 2007, the newly appointed Minister of Health became the first person to rise to ministerial rank without being a member of the Communist Party or any of the satellite parties loyal to the Communist Party. (Currently, the Minister of Science and Technology is the only other non-Communist Party minister in the State Council. He is, however, the chairman of one of the satellite parties, the Zhigong Party.) Advancement within China's civil service is generally based on performance, which is measured by how effectively civil servants carry out their responsibilities and achieve their specified goals, while avoiding scandal. As a result, one of the state's main means of political control is the evaluation of its personnel.

China's highest ranking state officials are the **State President** (*guojia zhuxi*) and **Vice President** (*guojia fuzhuxi*).[42] The positions are largely ceremonial and involve few duties. Since 1993, however, China's Communist Party General Secretaries have found it useful to serve concurrently as State President because General Secretaries have no counterparts outside the non-Communist world. When Hu Jintao traveled to the United States for a state visit in January 2011, he did so in his capacity as China's State President, although his real power derives from his position as General Secretary of the Communist Party. Xi Jinping traveled to the United States in February 2012 in his capacity as China's State Vice President, although his power derives from his position as the fifth ranked official on the Party's Politburo Standing Committee and from his status as Hu's heir apparent.

The locus of power in the State system is the **State Council**, China's cabinet. It is headed by a **Premier** *(zongli)*, also sometimes referred to in English as Prime Minister, who currently serves concurrently as the Communist Party's third-ranking official. Because the State system manages the economy on a day-to-day basis, the Premier is effectively China's most senior economic official, although he has many other portfolios, too. Below the Premier are four State Council **Vice Premiers**, who serve concurrently on the Communist Party Politburo, and five **State Councilors**, only one of whom serves on the Politburo. Each Vice Premier and State Councilor has a specific portfolio. China's most senior diplomat is a State Councilor, Dai Bingguo, who oversees the Ministry of Foreign Affairs and serves as office director for the Party's Foreign Affairs Leading Small Group.

---

[41] For more information about the establishment of the state system as a separate political institution, see Zhou Guanghui, "Towards Good Government: Thirty Years of Administrative Reforms in China," in *The Reform of Governance*, ed. Yu Keping (Leiden, The Netherlands and Beijing, China: Koninklijke Brill NV and Social Sciences Academic Press, 2010), pp. 137-180.

[42] A literal translation for the Chinese names, 主席 and 副主席, would be "chairman" and "vice chairman," but China's official translation is President and Vice President.

The **full State Council** is currently composed of the Premier, Vice Premiers, State Councilors, the State Council Secretary General, plus the heads of government ministries and commissions, the governor of China's central bank, and China's auditor general. It usually meets as a body approximately every six months, although it met for only a single annual session in 2010 and 2011.[43] China's **ministries** and **commissions,** which are subordinate to the State Council, are a fractious, highly competitive group of institutions with sometimes overlapping jurisdiction. Ministries are headed by **Ministers** and commissions by **Chairmen.** Each ministry or commission has an embedded Communist Party committee that makes major decisions for the institution and oversees ideology and personnel matters. In most cases, the Minister or Chairman serves concurrently as the head of his institution's Communist Party committee. The current exceptions are the State Ethnic Affairs Commission, the Ministry of Foreign Affairs, the Ministry of Science and Technology, and the Ministry of Health, where the top State and Party jobs are held by different people.[44]

Despite their subordination to the State Council and CCP, and the CCP's role in appointing their leaders, the ministries can wield decisive tactical influence over policy by virtue of their role in drafting laws and regulations and implementing the sometimes ambiguous national policy goals set by top leaders. Since General Secretary Hu Jintao's 2006 call for "indigenous innovation" to be "the core of national competitiveness," for example, the Ministry of Industry and Information Technology (MIIT) has led the way in developing often controversial industrial policies and regulations to support domestic firms over their foreign rivals, fleshing out just what "indigenous innovation" means. MIIT's moves have included attempts to make a domestic technology the standard for 3G mobile telecommunications in China, to require that all new computers in China be sold with Chinese-made censorship software pre-installed, and to require preference for domestic suppliers in Chinese government procurement.[45] Not all ministries and commissions are created equal. MIIT and the National Development and Reform Commission, both considered "super-ministries," are more powerful in policy debates than other ministries, such as the relatively weak Ministry of Health.

Entities under the State Council include four State Council offices, each with its own professional staff. The **State Council's Legislative Affairs Office** (SCLAO) plays a frequently decisive role in the formulation of national regulations and laws. It drafts the government's legislative agenda on a year-to-year basis and then works with relevant government ministries and agencies to implement the agenda, including overseeing the drafting of regulations and laws.[46] (Regulations are promulgated by the State Council or by individual ministries. Laws must be passed by the

---

[43] A list of State Council meetings going back to 2003 can be found on the State Council's website at http://www.gov.cn/gjjg/2005-07/26/content_17197.htm.

[44] In the case of the Ministry of Science and Technology and the Ministry of Health, having separate minister and party secretaries is unavoidable as their ministers are not Communist Party members. For more discussion of these issues, see Peng Mei and Ge Qian, "Zhang Zhijun Appointed Secretary of Foreign Ministry Party Committee, First-ranking Vice Minister (张志军任外交部党委书记排名第一的副部长)," *Southern Metropolis News (南方都市报,* December 22, 2010.

[45] James McGregor, *China's Drive for Indigenous Innovation: A Web of Industrial Policies,* U.S. Chamber of Commerce, July 2010, http://www.uschamber.com/reports/chinas-drive-indigenous-innovation-web-industrial-policies. Barry Naughton, "China's Emergence from Economic Crisis," *China Leadership Monitor,* no. 29 (August 11, 2009), http://www.hoover.org/publications/china-leadership-monitor/article/5473.

[46] The Legislative Affairs Office is also responsible for advising the State Council on the legal implications of ratifying or participating in international treaties, for issuing legal interpretations of administration regulations, and for reviewing local regulations and ministerial and agency regulations for consistency with national-level laws and regulations and China's constitution. For more information, see the Legislative Affairs Office's Chinese-language website at http://www.chinalaw.gov.cn/article/jgzn/.

National People's Congress.) The **State Council's Hong Kong and Macao Affairs Office** advises the Chinese leadership on matters related to the two Special Administrative Regions, both of which returned to Chinese sovereignty in the 1990s after long periods as colonies of Britain and Portugal respectively. The other two offices are a Research Office and an Overseas Chinese Affairs Office.

The National People's Congress (NPC)

The third major political institution in China is the National People's Congress (NPC), China's unicameral national legislature. According to Article 57 of China's constitution, the NPC is "the highest organ of state power." The Constitution tasks the NPC with overseeing the Presidency, the State Council, the State Central Military Commission, the Supreme People's Court, and China's national level public prosecutor's office, the Supreme People's Procuratorate. In practice, however, the NPC's powers are severely limited, and the entire entity operates under the leadership of the Communist Party.

The public theater of the NPC's work is centered around its ten-day-long annual full session, held every March and attended by all of the NPC's nearly 3,000 deputies. The next full session, in March 2013, will mark the start of a new five-year Congress, and is expected to approve a major leadership transition, including a new President and Premier, and new Vice Premiers and State Councilors. At the annual full sessions, NPC deputies almost always vote to approve the reports, laws, and candidates put before them, usually by overwhelming margins, leading many observers to describe the NPC as a "rubber stamp" parliament. NPC delegates do occasionally push back, however. At the March 2012 session of the NPC, for example, a record 20% of deputies withheld their support from the Ministry of Finance's budget report, reportedly in protest over the Ministry's longstanding refusal to accept any NPC suggestions for revisions to the budget.[47] (Unlike the U.S. Congress, the National People's Congress does not pass spending bills. Rather, at the annual full session each year, it votes to approve the budget presented by the Minister of Finance.) The NPC also makes revisions to the Premier's annual report on the work of the government, the State's most important policy document.

Out of the public eye, individual committees and the Standing Committee exercise more meaningful influence. They shape legislation and can exercise a degree of oversight over government entities through "inspection" visits and committee reports. The power of individual NPC deputies to exercise oversight is largely restricted to the right to submit "proposals" advocating for reforms or demanding better implementation of laws or regulations, to which officials are required to respond in writing.

Because the annual full session of the congress is so brief, much of the NPC's work is undertaken by its approximately 175-member **Standing Committee,** which meets about half a dozen times a year.[48] Other important NPC bodies include nine specialized committees and a legislative affairs work committee, all of which review and revise draft legislation before sending it to the Standing Committee or the full Congress for action. Like the State Council, the NPC has a Party

---

[47] See, for example, Wang Biqiang and Zheng Meng, "今年人大预算报告反对票数创记录 审议频遭冷场" (Opposing Votes for the Budget Report at this Year's NPC Set a Record: Review Frequently Meets with Awkward Silence), *Caijing*, 2012 Issue 9, March 26, 2012, http://news.hexun.com/2012-03-26/139730819.html.

[48] For a list of National People's Congress Standing Committee meetings since 2004, see the NPC's Chinese-language website: http://www.npc.gov.cn/npc/cwhhy/node_2433.htm.

---

organization embedded within it. The NPC's chairman serves on the Politburo Standing Committee and is currently the Party's number-two ranked official.

NPC deputies are not directly elected. The Communist Party draws up lists of nominees, based in part on potential nominees' perceived loyalty to the Party. Thirty-five electoral units, most of them provincial-level People's Congresses, then vote upon the Party's nominees. The process is modestly competitive in that the Party nominates 20% to 50% more candidates than available positions and those with the most votes are elected to serve as NPC deputies. NPC election rules stipulate quotas for the representation of ethnic minority groups, the military, women, and other groups, including the Party itself. Because China rejects any separation of powers, the President, Premier, and other top leaders are all NPC deputies.[49] Deputies serve for five-year terms.

The NPC is the uppermost layer of a nation-wide system of People's Congresses. These congresses are loosely linked together in process and function. Only deputies for the lowest level of People's Congresses are directly elected. Traditionally, even at the lowest level, candidate lists are controlled by the Party, and elections are uncontested. Since 2011, however, China has seen a wave of independent candidates contesting elections for People's Congresses in city districts and townships. Most such candidates have faced forms of official harassment, including intrusive surveillance, extra-legal detention, intimidation of their supporters, and election irregularities designed to keep them from appearing on ballots, but some have succeeded in being elected to office.[50]

The Chinese People's Political Consultative Conference (CPPCC)

The Chinese People's Political Consultative Conference (CPPCC) system officially exists to engage in "political consultation" with the Communist Party, perform "democratic supervision" of the Party, and "participate in the deliberation and administration of state affairs." The Communist Party routinely holds up the PPCC system as a core part of China's "socialist democracy," characterized by "multi-party cooperation and political consultation led by the Communist Party of China."[51] In practice, the CPPCC system gives select prominent citizens, many of them non-Communists, an approved platform to make suggestions about aspects of public policy, but does not oblige the Communist Party to act upon those suggestions. The institution can thus ignite and influence policy debates, but is essentially powerless. The Chinese government refers to CPPCC members as "political advisors."

The Minor Political Parties

As mentioned above, in addition to the Chinese Communist Party, China has eight other minor political parties. Their role is strictly circumscribed, but the Communist Party uses their existence to argue that China operates a "multi-party cooperation system," and is therefore not strictly a

---

[49] Jiang Jinsong, *The National People's Congress of China* (Foreign Languages Press Beijing, 2003), pp. 86-104.

[50] For details of the sort of harassment faced by independent candidates, see the tale of Liu Ping, a thwarted candidate for municipal People's Congress in Jiangxi Province. Liu Chang, "Why Liu Ping's Candidacy Failed," *Caixin Online*, June 7, 2011, http://english.caixin.com/2011-06-07/100266830.html

[51] National Committee of the Chinese People's Political Consultative Conference, *Nature and Position of the CPPCC*, June 29, 2010, http://www.cppcc.gov.cn.

one-party state.[52] Crucially, the minor political parties are all required to accept the permanent leadership of the Communist Party. They are expected to work "hand in hand" with the Communist Party in "developing socialism with Chinese characteristics," and they are barred from operating as opposition parties. The combined members of the minor parties number fewer than one million, compared to the Communist Party's 80 million members, with the smallest of the parties claiming a membership of just 2,100. The minor parties exercise modest influence in the political system by virtue of the Communist Party's policy of allotting leadership positions for the minor parties' members in the state bureaucracy, the legislatures, and the political advisory bodies. The heads of the minor parties all serve as vice-chairmen of the National People's Congress, making them state leaders for protocol purposes. In 2007, the current Minister of Science and Technology, Wan Gang, became the first minor party member in the post-Mao era to be named to a ministerial post. He serves concurrently as chairman of the Zhi Gong Party, whose mandate is to represent Chinese who have returned to China after living overseas or who have relatives living overseas.[53]

Other Political Actors

In addition to the formal institutions of government and party power, the PRC political system is increasingly influenced by other political actors, sometimes referred to as "policy entrepreneurs."[54] Some of these influential actors operate opaquely and behind the scenes, making it difficult to determine the exact extent of their influence on any given policy issue. Others are playing an increasingly visible role in debating, recommending, and influencing particular policy actions. The media plays an important role in amplifying the voices of the other actors.

Traditional Media, New Media, and a Wired Citizenry

Control of the media has always been an important plank of Communist Party rule in China, enabling the Party to "guide public opinion" with its version of events, and to exclude narratives that might challenge Party positions or actions. Party media controls remain in place, but with the reduction of state subsidies to the traditional media, the rise of commercially driven media, and the rapid spread of new information technologies, the Chinese media landscape has become increasingly diverse, eroding the Party's ability to control public discourse as comprehensively as it once did.

Traditional, tightly controlled Communist Party media outlets, such as the Communist Party Central Committee's *People's Daily*, now co-exist with more lively commercially driven

---

[52] For more information about the minor political parties, see State Council Information Office of the People's Republic of China, *China's Political Party System*, White Paper, Beijing, China, November 2007, http://english.people.com.cn/90001/90776/90785/6303123.html.

[53] The eight minor parties are the Revolutionary Committee of the Chinese Kuomintang (RCCK), China Democratic League (CDL), China National Democratic Construction Association (CNDCA), China Association for Promoting Democracy (CAPD), Chinese Peasants and Workers Democratic Party (CPWDP), China Zhi Gong Dang (CZGD), Jiu San Society, and Taiwan Democratic Self-Government League (TSL).

[54] For discussion of the role of policy entrepreneurs in Chinese policymaking, see Andrew Mertha, "'Fragmented Authoritarianism 2.0': Political Pluralization in the Chinese Policy Process," *The China Quarterly*, no. 200 (December 2009).

publications. Such publications put a provocative spin on Party-approved news, expose scandals, and report on policy debates, even though they may share the same owners as staid Party papers and are also subject to Party Propaganda Department censorship. One of China's most feisty tabloids, the *Global Times*, is a sister paper to the *People's Daily*. The crusading *Southern Metropolis News* and *Southern Weekend*, both known for their daring investigative journalism, are sister papers to the mouthpiece of the Guangdong Communist Party Committee, *Southern Daily*. China's financial media, which tend to be less tightly censored than the mainstream media, often showcase some of the most probing analysis of policy issues, with publications such as *Caixin New Century Weekly* and *Caijing* being particularly closely read by elites. Because of its reach, television is the most tightly controlled medium in China. China Central Television (CCTV), which operates multiple channels on multiple platforms, serves as a tool of the Communist Party, relaying Party-approved messages to China's citizens. It also, however, hosts numerous talk shows and magazine-style programs that offer a range of opinions on policy issues.

The most significant development in the media landscape in recent years has been the explosive growth of Twitter-like services known as "weibo" (literally micro-blogs), which have empowered citizens to share news and views directly with each other, and thus put pressure on the traditional media to cover stories they might otherwise have ignored, and on the authorities to address problems they might otherwise have swept under the carpet. Some micro-bloggers have millions of followers and the power to change the terms of public debate with a single post. As of January 2012, nearly 40% of Chinese were online, with the total number of internet users reaching 513 million. Nearly 70% of Chinese users accessed the internet on mobile devices, and 250 million Chinese were weibo users.[55] Authorities police weibo posts. In the wake of the scandal involving the former Party Secretary of Chongqing, they boasted of deleting 210,000 weibo posts and making six arrests for online "rumor mongering."[56] In an attempt to turn weibo to the Party's advantage, however, the CCP has also encouraged official agencies and officials to open weibo accounts as a new tool in their propaganda toolboxes, and the official Xinhua News Agency now releases news on weibo as well as on its other platforms. Many Chinese officials monitor weibo and other Internet discussions as a guide to public opinion, even though in China, as in many societies, extreme views tend to dominate Internet-based discourse. Chinese officials sometimes tell foreign officials about the pressure they feel from the nationalist views of China's "netizens," suggesting that it may be a factor in Chinese foreign policy.

Big Business

Boosted by government policies restricting foreign investment and private investment in "strategic industries," flagship Chinese state-owned enterprises (SOE's) in such fields as oil, electric power, finance, telecommunications, and defense have emerged as global powerhouses in recent years. (Three Chinese SOE's are among the top 10 firms on the Fortune Global 500 list for 2011.[57]) The leaders of such firms, and indeed all Chinese SOEs, are assigned to their jobs by the Party's Organization Department and thus may move back and forth between jobs in business and

---

[55] China Internet Network Information Center, 中国互联网络发展状况统计报告 (*Statistical Report on Internet Development in China*), January 2012, pp. 4-5, http://www.cnnic.com.cn/dtygg/dtgg/201201/W020120116337628870651.pdf.

[56] Liu Yang, "清理21万条信息 关闭42家网站 (Cleaned Up 210,000 Posts; Closed 42 Websites)," *The People's Daily*, April 13, 2012, http://paper.people.com.cn/rmrb/html/2012-04/13/nw.D110000renmrb_20120413_1-04.htm.

[57] The three are Sinopec Group, China National Petroleum Corporation, and State Grid Corporation of China, ranked 5th, 6th, and 7th, respectively. CNN Money, *Global 500*, 2011, http://money.cnn.com/magazines/fortune/global500/2011/full_list/.

government, and have a formal place in the Chinese political system. Twenty-two SOE bosses are currently alternate members of the Party's Central Committee, and one is a full member.[58]

Analysts say SOE bosses are able to influence policymaking and agenda-setting by virtue of their bureaucratic rank, their technical knowledge of their industries and global markets, and the economic might of their firms. With their career advancement in the Party's hands, however, SOE bosses understand that they are expected not just to produce strong corporate results, but also to ensure that their firms advance the Party's interests.[59]

The leaders of the largest private firms are outside the Party's personnel assignment system, but are often also significant players in the Chinese political system. One scholar identifies property developers, a group that includes both private and state-owned giants, as "one of the most powerful special interest groups in present-day China," blaming it for holding up passage of an anti-monopoly law and resisting government efforts to rein in a dangerous property bubble.[60] Lu Guanqiu, founder of auto-parts giant Wanxiang, was a member of the business delegation that accompanied Vice President Xi Jinping on a visit to the United States in February 2012 and attended a meeting Vice President Biden and Treasury Secretary Timothy Geithner.[61]

The Party has routinely awarded prominent businesspeople, from both state-owned and privately-owned firms, positions as deputies to national and local congresses and Political Consultative Conferences. According to Bloomberg News, as of 2011, the richest 70 delegates to the National People's Congress had a combined net worth of $89.8 billion.[62] In 2002, the Party formally welcomed private business leaders into its ranks.

---

[58] Erica Downs and Michal Meidan, "Business and Politics in China: The Oil Executive Reshuffle of 2011," *China Security*, no. 19 (2011), pp. 3-21.

[59] Ibid.

[60] Cheng Li, "China's Midterm Jockeying: Gearing Up for 2012 (Part 4: Top Leaders of Major State-Owned Enterprises)," *China Leadership Monitor*, no. 34 (February 22, 2011), http://www.hoover.org/publications/china-leadership-monitor/article/68001.

[61] Michael Forsythe, "China's Billionaire People's Congress Makes Capitol Hill Look Like Pauper," *Bloomberg News*, February 27, 2012.

[62] Ibid.

Official and Quasi-Official Research Institutes

According to a recent University of Pennsylvania global ranking that has been embraced in China, the country now has 425 think tanks, the second largest number in the world after the United States, with six Chinese think tanks ranked among the top 30 in Asia.[63] With "think tank" a relatively new term in China, introduced from the West, most of the institutions on the list would be better known in China as public policy **research institutes**. Many are affiliated either with an official agency (such as the Ministry of State Security's China Institutes for Contemporary International Relations, widely known as CICIR) or a university (such as Peking University's Center for Strategic and International Studies.) Such centers make their influence felt in the policy process in part by accepting commissions from the Party or state to write reports on policy issues, and by self-generating reports that they submit to policymakers. Experts attached to the institutes also often serve as formal and informal advisors to official bodies, publish broadly, and may maintain a domestic media profile, accepting interviews, participating in television chat shows, and penning media commentaries. Such experts also play an important role in informing the outside world about Chinese policy discourse through meetings at home and abroad with foreign scholars, officials, and visitors from the U.S. Congress, as well as through attendance at international conferences and publications in international journals.

Top-Ranked Chinese Think Tanks

Chinese Academy of Social Sciences (No. 28 among think tanks globally, No. 14 among non-U.S. think tanks globally, and No. 1 in Asia)

China Institutes of Contemporary International Relations (No. 42 among non-U.S. think tanks globally and No. 6 in Asia)

Shanghai Institute for International Studies (No. 8 in Asia)

Center for International and Strategic Studies at Peking University (No. 19 in Asia)

Cathay Institute for Public Affairs (No. 27 in Asia)

Carnegie-Tsinghua Institute for Global Policy (No. 28 in Asia)

China Center for International Economic Exchanges (No. 3 among new think tanks globally)

Brookings-Tsinghua Center for Public Policy (No. 14 among university-affiliated think tanks globally)

Institute for International Relations, Tsinghua University (No. 25 among university-affiliated think tanks globally)

China Institute of International Studies (No. 18 among government-affiliated think tanks globally)

Central Party School (No. 17 among party-affiliated think tanks globally)

Unirule Institute of Economics (No. 12 among think tanks globally with operating budgets of less than $5 million/year)

Source: University of Pennsylvania, *The Global Go To Think Tanks Report 2011*, January 20, 2012.

Notably, all of the Chinese think tanks named in the University of Pennsylvania survey are located in either Beijing or Shanghai, the two cities that dominate the policy discourse in China. Only one of the Chinese think tanks named in the rankings could be described as independent (Unirule Institute of Economics), and it is in the category of think tanks with small budgets.

---

[63] James G. McGann, PhD, *The Global Go To Think Tanks Report 2011*, Think Tanks and Civil Societies Program, International Relations Program, University of Pennsylvania, January 20, 2012, http://www.gotothinktank.com/wp-content/uploads/2012/01/2011-Global-Go-To-Think-Tanks-Report.pdf.

University Academics

China's academic community includes more than 1,100 degree-granting institutions.[64] Their faculty, even if not attached to policy research institutes, may be players in policy debates as authors of reports and influential articles and books, as government advisors, and as media commentators. More than four dozen Chinese universities are under the management of the military or central government ministries other than the Ministry of Education; many of them have a direct line into policy as a result.[65] In a well respected annual ranking of China's top 50 universities carried out by China Renmin University (see accompanying text box), four of the top ten universities are based in Beijing and two in Shanghai. Institutions in Hangzhou, Nanjing, Hefei, and Tianjin round out the top ten.[66] Notably, universities in China are not independent. They have Communist Party committees that act like Party Committees in other institutions, making

China's Top Ranked Universities

1. Peking University (Beijing)

2. Tsinghua University (Beijing)

3. Fudan University (Shanghai)

4. China Renmin University (Beijing)

5. Zhejiang University (Hangzhou)

6. Nanjing University (Nanjing)

7. China University of Science and Technology (Hefei)

8. Shanghai Jiaotong University (Shanghai)

9. Beijing Normal University (Beijing)

10. Nankai University (Tianjin)

Source: China Renmin University Higher Education Research Center, *2011 Chinese Universities Top 50 Rankings: China Renmin University Edition*, June 14, 2011.

major decisions for the university and managing ideology, personnel, propaganda, and financial matters. As noted above, 32 universities have quasi ministerial bureaucratic rank. (See "The Distorting Influence of Bureaucratic Rank.")

Officially-Sponsored Associations and Societies

China has 1,800 officially-registered national-level "social organizations" (*shehui tuanti*), the bulk of which are what Western scholars refer to as GONGOs, or "government-organized non-government organizations."[67] Some such organizations have been criticized as little more than retirement homes for officials who have had to leave office because of age limits. Others, however, play an influential role. The fact that GONGO leaders are usually recently retired senior officials means that they have status and deep relationships in government that can make them effective bureaucratic players. Under-staffed ministries and Communist Party departments often outsource parts of their work to GONGOs, from drafting standards and staffing legislative drafting committees, to organizing conferences. GONGOs also sometimes act as proxies for the

---

[64] The number of degree-granting institutions at the end of 2010 was 1,112. Ministry of Education of the People's Republic of China, 中国教育概况 2010年全国教育事业发展情况 (*General Information About Chinese Education: 2010 National Situation of Development in the Education Field*), November 14, 2011, http://www.moe.edu.cn/publicfiles/business/htmlfiles/moe/s5990/201111/126550.html.

[65] A list of universities affiliated with central government ministries and commissions is available on the website of the *People's Daily*, at http://edu.people.gkcx.eol.cn/schoolInfoSearch/zybw/zybw_1.htm.

[66] China Renmin University Higher Education Research Center, *2011 Chinese Universities Top 50 Rankings: China Renmin University Edition*, June 14, 2011, http://edu.people.com.cn/GB/14894813.html.

[67] For statistics on social organizations, see Ministry of Civil Affairs, 2009 年民政事业发展统计报告 (2009 Civil Affairs Development Statistical Report), April 6, 2011, accessible at http://www.chinanpo.gov.cn/web/showBulltetin.do?id=48276&dictionid=2201&catid=.

government at international meetings. The number of GONGOs that each agency sponsors varies. The Foreign Ministry sponsors 14, including the China Arms Control and Disarmament Association, a frequent participant in international arms control dialogues. The Ministry of Industry and Information Technology sponsors 41, many of them industry associations that bring perspectives from corporate leaders to bear on policy issues.[68]

Grassroots NGOs

Grassroots non-governmental organizations (NGOs) also exist in China, although in most of the country, to be officially registered as NGOs they need to find a government department willing to serve as their sponsor. (Guangdong Province is the first to experiment with a policy of waiving this requirement.) Unable to line up sponsors, many grassroots NGOs are forced to register as businesses. Despite official obstacles, which include harassment from China's security apparatus, a number of grassroots NGOs have been successful in raising public awareness about such issues as environmental protection and public health and in providing services to under-served populations, such as the disabled. The Beijing Yirenping Center, for example, focuses on combating discrimination on the basis of health status or disability. Yirenping's advocacy has involved exploiting openings in the Chinese political system to draw attention to its causes, usually with the help of sympathetic journalists. Among other tactics, it has launched lawsuits, filed official information disclosure requests, organized petitions and open letters, and persuaded People's Congress and People's Political Consultative Conference delegates to submit proposals on their behalf calling for revision of laws discriminating against such groups as carriers of Hepatitis B and HIV.[69]

Chinese Authorities' View of Political Reform

China's Premier Wen Jiabao, who is scheduled to retire from his Party posts later this year and from the premiership in March 2013, has made tantalizing comments over the years about the need for political reform in China. In an unusual 2008 interview with the U.S. network CNN, Wen spoke of the need "to gradually improve the democratic election system," "build an independent and just judicial system," and have the government "accept oversight by the news media and other parties."[70] In a second interview with CNN in 2010, Wen declared that "freedom of speech is indispensable," and that "All political parties, organizations, and all people should abide by the constitution and laws without any exception."[71] Most recently, at what was likely his last press conference as Premier, given to mark the closing of the annual full session of the National People's Congress in March 2012, Wen spoke of the need for "political structural

---

[68] GONGOs can be searched by sponsoring agency on the website of the Chinese Ministry of Civil Affairs, using a Chinese-language search platform accessed at http://www.chinanpo.gov.cn/npowork/dc/searchOrgList.do?action= searchOrgList..

[69] For examples of recent Yirenping activism, see *Many Activities on Human Rights of People with Disability were carried out at the Beginning of 2012*, Beijing Yirenping report, January 30, 2012, http://www.asiacatalyst.org/blog/ 2012/02/Yirenping_Center_Reports_On_Disability_Action.pdf.

[70] CNN, *Fareed Zakaria GPS: Interviews with Wen Jiabao, Malcolm Gladwell*, August 23 2009, http://transcripts.cnn.com/TRANSCRIPTS/0908/23/fzgps.01.html. (The Wen interview originally aired on September 29, 2008. The August 23, 2009, edition of Fareed Zakaria GPS re-broadcast the interview.)

[71] CNN, *Fareed Zakaria GPS: Interview with Wen Jiabao*, October 3, 2010, http://transcripts.cnn.com/ TRANSCRIPTS/1010/03/fzgps.01.html.

---

reform," and particularly of the need for "reform in the leadership system of the Party and the state," although he did not clarify what kind of reform the "leadership system" needed. He also startled journalists by embracing the Arab spring, declaring that, "The Arab people's demand and pursuit of democracy must be respected and realistically answered. Further, I feel that this trend of democracy is unstoppable by any forces."[72]

No other senior leaders have echoed Wen's call for judicial independence or for the Communist Party to be bound "without any exception" by the constitution and laws, however, and the substance of Wen's remarks to CNN has never been reported in the Chinese media.[73] Reflecting the diversity of views among top leaders, other top party officials have instead insisted on the limits of political reform in China. In widely reported remarks to the annual full session of the National People's Congress in March 2011, Wu Bangguo, the NPC Chairman and the Communist Party's number two-ranked official, reinforced the Party's insistence on its permanent, unchallenged rule by declaring that China's leaders had "made a solemn declaration that we'll not employ a system of multiple parties holding office in rotation." He also foreswore any separation of executive, legislative, and judicial powers, and any adoption of a bicameral or federal system, warning that China would risk an "abyss of internal disorder" if it deviated from the "correct political orientation."[74] The views of those who will step into top leadership positions at the 18th Party Congress in late 2012 remain unknown.

The Communist Party's Propaganda Department has been active in justifying harder line positions. In a 2009 political tract, *Six 'Why's': Answers to Some Major Questions*, it took on such questions as, "Why must we uphold the system of multi-party cooperation and political consultation under the leadership of the Chinese Communist Party, and not have a Western-style multi-party system?" Many of the answers the book offered focused on claims that Western political systems are inefficient and unable to deliver the kind of fast-paced economic growth that China needs to pull all its people out of poverty. Among the many ills associated with competitive two-party or multi-party politics, the book argued, are deepened social divisions and an unstable political situation, which hobbles economic development. Separation of powers is not for China, the book declared, because it results in different power centers going their own ways and failing to pull together to resolve major problems facing the country, leading to the public's loss of faith in government. The book offered as evidence for this particular thesis the U.S. government shutdown of 1995, and subsequent threats of U.S. government shutdowns.[75]

While the Communist Party has shown little no interest in reforms that might threaten its monopoly on power, for most of the last 30 years it has been undertaking what a leading Chinese political scientist, Yu Keping, calls "reform of state governance and the administrative systems of the state," intended to improve China's governance in ways that might help solidify the Party's hold on power.[76] Recent efforts have focused on ways of increasing the legitimacy of the political

[72] Ministry of Foreign Affairs of the People's Republic of China, "Premier Wen Jiabao Meets the Press," transcript, March 15, 2012, http://www.fmprc.gov.cn/eng/zxxx/t914983.htm.

[73] For discussion of Wen's remarks and their reporting in China, see Alice L. Miller, "Splits in the Politburo Leadership?" and Joseph Fewsmith, "Political Reform Was Never on the Agenda," *China Leadership Monitor*, no. 34 (February 22, 2011), http://www.hoover.org/publications/china-leadership-monitor/article/67996.

[74] Bao Daozu, "Top Legislator Warns of Chaos Unless Correct Path Is Taken," *China Daily*, March 11, 2011, online edition, http://www.chinadaily.com.cn/china/2011npc/2011-03/11/content_12152319.htm.

[75] Theory Bureau of the Communist Party Central Committee Propaganda Department, 六个为什么：对几个重大问题的回答 *(Six 'Why's': Answers to Some Major Questions)* (Beijing, China: Xuexi Chubanshe, 2009), pp. 73, 56-57.

[76] Yu Keping, "30 Years of China's Governance Reform (1978 to 2008)," in *The Reform of Governance*, ed. Yu (continued...)

system by making it more competitive, transparent, and participatory, without going so far as to cede the Party's ultimate control over all major decisions.

In the 1980s, in an effort to foster greater support for local leaders among the community, create incentives for more effective local governance, and provide a disincentive for local government corruption, the Party sanctioned limited direct elections for leaders at level of the village, an administrative unit outside the formal Chinese administrative hierarchy. Those elections continue, although it is important to note that village party officials, who are not subject to popular vote, determine what name or names may appear on the ballot, and that the rules bar candidates from running on behalf of a political party or as part of a slate of candidates and restrict public campaigning to a few minutes of public remarks immediately before the vote. In his March 2012 press conference, Premier Wen pronounced village elections a success and said he saw no reason why such direct elections could not eventually move up to the level of the township, and even the county.[77]

More recent innovations include efforts to introduce elections on a limited scope in workplaces.[78] The Party has also introduced public hearings, begun posting select draft legislation for public comment, and adopted a set of open government information regulations to improve the transparency of government. Comprehensive ministerial and provincial government websites are a product of this initiative.[79] Although the Party has touted these and other political reforms with great fanfare, they have their limitations and appear to be designed to head off demands for Chinese citizens to have a direct role in selecting their top leaders, rather than to pave the way for citizens to claim such a role.

Author Contact Information

Susan V. Lawrence
Specialist in Asian Affairs
slawrence@crs.loc.gov, 7-2577

Michael F. Martin
Specialist in Asian Affairs
mfmartin@crs.loc.gov, 7-2199

Acknowledgments

Kerry Dumbaugh was an author on the original version of this report. She left CRS at the end of December 2009.

(...continued)

Keping (Koninklijke Brill NV and Social Sciences Academic Press, 2010), pp. 4-14.

[77] Ministry of Foreign Affairs of the People's Republic of China, "Premier Wen Jiabao Meets the Press," transcript, March 15, 2012, http://www.fmprc.gov.cn/eng/zxxx/t914983.htm.

[78] For more information on China's experiments with "intra-Party democracy," see Cheng Li, "Intra-Party Democracy in China: Should We Take It Seriously?" *China Leadership Monitor*, no. 30 (November 19, 2009), http://www.hoover.org/publications/china-leadership-monitor/article/5413.

[79] The China Law Center at Yale Law School maintains a useful website with links to the full texts of China's open government information regulations in both English and Chinese: http://www.law.yale.edu/intellectuallife/openinformation.htm.